To:

May continue to rest upon you and guide your every step.

God's Blessings

Charles A. Hall
8/021

Real Faith

Real Faith

Growing In Faith While Enduring Life's Challenges

Pastor Charles A. Hall

XULON PRESS

Xulon Press
2301 Lucien Way #415
Maitland, FL 32751
407.339.4217
www.xulonpress.com

Unless otherwise indicated, Scripture quotations taken
from the King James Version (KJV) – *public domain*.

PAPERBACK ISBN-13: 978-1-6312-9385-6

EBOOK ISBN-13: 978-1-6312-9386-3

Endorsements

This book is a must-read for anyone who might benefit from the sharing of one of God's servant's innermost feelings during a time of personal struggle. This writing reflects the deep feeling of the author and the transformation that has taken place in him as he has sought and received a greater presence of God in his life. I have witnessed my husband's spiritual growth during one of the most trying times of his life, and he never wavered or doubted the power of God.

Ruby Worthy-Hall (Wife)

We have witnessed firsthand the spiritual strength and dedication of the author, our father, Pastor Charles A. Hall. Our father has always been our earthly role model, so it was not a surprise that he would trust God in whatever situation he might face in his life's journey. We have seen up close how our father has grown spiritually as he has been challenged physically, without wavering at any time. If you want to meet an ordinary God-fearing man who believes and trusts in the supernatural power of a loving God, then this book is a must-read!

Devin, Brian, NyKia, and NyJuan (Children)

Dear Reader, this book is a must-read. Since **our** brother, Pastor Charles, started writing, he has always invited his readers to join him on his journey—a journey of challenges, forgiveness, hope, obedience, trust in God, and reward! This book is a beacon of hope for those who may be struggling with holding on to their passion for life! This book tells the unique story of Pastor Charles's challenges, and more important, this book tells how his strong faith in God has made him a strong warrior on the battlefield for Christ. On behalf of Charles's siblings, thank you for taking the time to read **our** brother's book. We pray it will encourage you, lift you up to greater heights, and inspire you to "Hold on to God's Unchanging Hands!" ***But by the grace of God!***

Dr. Deborah Hall-Thomas, PhD (Sister)

Dedication

I dedicate this book to my family: to my wife, Ruby, and our four children: Devin, Brian, NyKia, NyJuan and their families, who besides the Lord have been my primary sources of strength and inspiration over the years. This book is dedicated to my siblings, who have motivated and encouraged me throughout my life. This book is also dedicated to my St. John Baptist Church family, who loves me and prays for me every day. And finally, I dedicate this book to all those who may be facing uncertain challenges in their lives.

Charles A. Hall

Table of Contents

Foreword

*C*harles *Alvin Hall*, successful and lauded corporate executive, entrepreneur, philanthropist, hometown sports legend, preacher of the Gospel, loving pastor, missionary, lover of the people of God, steadfast practitioner of the faith, committed husband, father extraordinaire, bond-servant of Jesus, the living Christ, *is my friend*!

I open my comments about this, his most recent commentary on life, because these words describe my brother's passion and excellence for life. He has never been a man to boast of perfection, but his passion and excellence for life in Christ have always driven his boundless energy in his pursuit of it. You may not agree with every word or idea that my friend presents in this treatise of his life, but you won't deny his passion, nor will you deny his committed pursuit of excellence in Christ.

I will never forget the night that he called (smitten with humility) and informed me that he had experienced the calling to preach and much later the call to pastor. I knew that his previous passion and excellence for life had been arrested, recalibrated, and refocused for . . . well, let my friend complete my point as given him by the apostle Paul:

> *[7] And lest I should be exalted above measure through the abundance of the revelations, there was given to me a thorn in the flesh, the messenger of Satan to buffet me, lest I should be exalted above measure. [8] For this thing I besought the Lord thrice, that it might depart from me. [9] And he said unto me, My grace is sufficient for thee:* **for my strength is made perfect in weakness. Most gladly therefore will I rather glory in my infirmities, that the power of Christ may rest upon me.**

Read with interest about the journey of my brother's passion and excellence for life, but redefined/sanctified by and to the glory of his new overseer, Jesus, the Christ, his never-ending source. My prayer is that after you read this life-altering testimony of Charles *"Growing in Faith While Enduring Life's Challenges,"* you will come away desiring more of what redefined passion and excellence of life for him.

Reverend Garfield Cross III
(A Co-Laborer and Observing Friend on the Journey)

Preface

I t is my sincere hope and prayer that all who read this book will be encouraged—not by the trials and challenges mentioned but by the way life is being embraced through these trying times. And the rewards of remaining well rooted and steadfast in a relationship with our Savior, Jesus Christ. This book references the testimony of one of God's earthly servants—me—who is far from perfect but learning how to embrace and trust God in whatever state I may be.

This book is written from a personal perspective that represents a major challenge for me. I am not a person who by nature is comfortable sharing information regarding such a personal matter. However, the Holy Spirit has given me spiritual boldness and personal liberty to share my situation and my feelings. This is such a paradigm shift for me, which is confirmation that writing this book represents a move of God in my life. I constantly asked God through prayer to give me the strength to finish and release this manuscript.

Writing this book was not something I *wanted* to do; it was something I *felt compelled* to do.

It is my sincere hope and prayer that my sharing might help someone who may be facing a similar challenge in his or her life, regardless of the type of challenge, whether health, mental, relational, or any other personal trial. It is also my prayer that those who read this book will be encouraged and uplifted by the abundant amount of grace God has bestowed on me, with the belief that if God could do this for me, then He can do it for you as well.

Let me make this as clear as possible: this book is not being written to seek sympathy or pity; on the contrary, it is my hope and prayer that this book will give the reader hope, joy, and the peace of God. There is nothing I am seeking from anyone; God has given me everything I need. In fact, He has far exceeded my needs. I am in good health; by the grace of God, I have been given an extremely high energy level for a seventy-year-old man. I feel as strong today as I felt ten years ago. *I think I have found a spiritual fountain of youth.*

Acknowledgments

My Wife, Ruby

I must take this opportunity to thank my wife, Ruby, who has been the love of my life for more than fifty years; she is the mother of my children, my best friend, and my earthly soulmate. The Lord has used Ruby to give deeper meaning to my life; her unwavering support and dedication to the call of God upon my life is unquestionable. She is my earthly inspiration; she has always supported my ministry, even during the difficult and challenging times. I could not have written this book without the support and encouragement from my wife. God used her to motivate me to share this season of my life with others. I thank God for creating her just for me!

My Family

My family has always been a source of strength and inspiration for me, especially in my ministry. They have stood side by side with me, not just during this season but always. They pray for me, they encourage me, and most importantly, they believe in the God that I serve and have fostered their own relationship with Christ. For this I am most grateful.

Introduction

I am blessed beyond measure that the Holy Spirit has enabled me to write and publish two books before this one: first, *Being a Prayer Warrior*, and later, *Breaking Spiritual Strongholds by the Word of God*. Late in 2018, while being led by the Holy Spirit, I was moved to write and publish my third book, the one you are reading now: *Real Faith*. I must admit I was very excited to be called to write about faith.

Shortly after I started writing what I believed at the time was a generic book about faith using the Word of God as the foundation, I was diagnosed with severe advanced cancer stage 4. The news and the following treatments halted my writing completely. For most of 2019, I did not write anything for this book; I wanted to write, but I found it difficult to put pen to paper. I fasted and prayed that the Lord would give me the motivation and desire to write again. Then one day in late November 2019, the Holy Spirit spoke to my spirit; it was as clear as an audible voice speaking to me. The Holy Spirit told me it was time to write again and that God had provided me with the subject matter for my writing.

After much prayer and fasting, I realized that I had been given the writing assignment by God prior to the revealing of the subject matter. Since He is God, He knew the subject matter in advance of the assignment. When I was called to write this book, I had no idea that I would be writing about myself. Now that I clearly understand what my assignment is, I am appreciative that I was called to write this book prior to the Holy Spirit revealing its subject matter. If I had known the subject matter when I first began writing, I may never have fully embraced the assignment. It may have been too difficult to process, since I needed time to understand and gauge this sudden and unexpected turn in my life's journey. Especially since I did not see or anticipate this turn at all.

I could never have imagined cancer being a part of my life. My family has been blessed; I do not know of any immediate family member who has died from cancer or who is currently living with diagnosed cancer. So there was no forewarning! In fact, I did not miss any of my scheduled health exams or prescreening appointments over the years. Prior to receiving this alarming news, I had no idea I might have cancer. Now that I have educated myself as much as possible on the type of cancer that I have and have had the opportunity to more thoroughly review my prior years' prescreening test results, I have noticed an increase in one of the categories that could potentially indicate the possibility of early cancer. For whatever reason, these increases over the prior years never alarmed my primary care provider, thus no early biopsies were performed.

It would have been easy to blame someone for my health situation, but the truth is that God either caused it or allowed it to occur. So any questions I had needed to be addressed to God Himself. After seeking God in fervent prayer, I felt His voice speaking in my spirit, telling me that everything would be alright. I felt the presence of the Living God in my spirit declaring that this unexpected health situation would add spiritual value to my journey and my ministry. I heard God say that this battle was not mine but His. I felt in my spirit that all I had to do was just lean on and depend on God and everything would work itself out for my good. The doctors have indicated that it may take a couple of years or so to fully determine whether or not my cancer treatment plan worked. Regardless of what happens, I trust God and know in my heart that everything will work out for my good.

> *And we know that all things work together for good to them that love God, to them who are called according to his purpose.* **Romans 8:28**

A Season Of Maturity

This book is being written during a time in my life when my faith is being tested to a greater height than I have ever experienced before, and yet it has presented me with my greatest opportunity for maturity and growth in the Lord. I have learned that if we do not waver, we will eventually emerge from life's trials and challenges much stronger than we were when they first entered our life.

For some time now, I have considered myself to be a man of considerable faith; however, I really could not truthfully gauge the depth of my faith until I was presented with a situation that truly tested it in a way that it has never been tested before. I have felt my faith in God was strong during many difficult circumstances that I have had in my life. As a result, during these times of uncertainty, I was confident and completely dependent on God to handle or resolve whatever was going on in my life in a manner He felt would be best for me.

I knew the scripture, so I believed I understood what God wanted from me in those uncertain times in my life.

> Now faith is the substance of things hoped for, the evidence of things not seen. **Hebrews 11:1**

During those past difficulties in my life, it wasn't that I did not have true faith, but now I must confirm that my faith is strong enough in this current season to sustain me during this present crisis. Through these trials and challenges, God has reminded me many times that real faith is not static; rather it grows stronger and stronger as we mature in Christ. In my current season, I have been presented with a health crisis for which the probability of earthly healing is not real high. However, this human prognosis comes at a time when my faith is stronger and more resilient than ever before. I believe beyond a shadow of a doubt that my health crisis is not about me at all but rather is an opportunity for God to get His glory through my testimony during my personal time of struggle.

I am not saying I don't deserve what is happening to me, because I do; in fact, I deserve much worse: death. I know that I deserve death because the Word of God tells me that the wages of sin is death, and I have committed many sins in my lifetime. However, God also says that His gift to us is eternal life through Jesus Christ our Lord. During my lifetime, I have accepted without reservation God's gift of salvation based on my faith and my belief that He is exactly who He says He is and that He did everything He says He has done. I believe Jesus Christ is the Son of God; that He was born of a virgin; and that He gave His life on the cross for my sins, defeated death, rose again from the dead on the third day, then claimed His rightful place on the throne in heaven, next to God the Father. My unconditional love of God and my unwavering belief in the redeeming power of Jesus Christ gives me the strength to stand firm and victorious in the midst of my trials... because I know that greater is He that is in me than he that is in the world!

> *Ye are of God, little children, and have overcome them: because greater is he that is in you, than he that is in the world.* **1 John 4:4**

> *Nay, in all these things we are more than conquerors through him that loved us.* **Romans 8:37**

Real Faith

Real faith is when we as believers feel the presence of God in our lives. The stronger the presence of God, the greater our faith in Him. In chapter 14 of the gospel of John, in verses 15 through 28—with an emphasis on verse 23—God speaks through John to us about His presence in us. He says that if we love God, we will obey Him, and God will live in us.

> *Jesus answered and said unto him, if a man love me, he will keep my words: and my Father will love him, and we will come unto him, and make our abode with him.* ***John 14:23***

If real faith is the presence of God in our lives, then the lack of real faith is the absence of the presence of God in our lives. This condition occurs when we allow our flesh to dominate our decisions and our actions—in other words, when we're led by the flesh rather than by the spirit. Since the Holy Spirit is God, then the absence of His Spirit is the absence of the presence of God.

> *For here are three that bear record in heaven, the Father, the Word, and the Holy Ghost: and these three are one.*
> **1 John 5:7**

One benefit of going through my current trial is that it is presenting me with an opportunity to test my faith, to determine whether my faith is just words that flow out of my mouth or if my relationship with the Lord is truly based on real, undeniable faith. If my faith is made up of only words, my relationship with God will be exposed because I will start to turn to the world for answers and solutions, or to blame others for whatever is happening in my life; or I might just try to blame God. However, if my faith is real, and if I truly know who God is and what He has done for me—and if I truly love Him and have professed my desire to follow Him and Him only—then I know that no matter what I am going through or what my challenge is, it will eventually work out for my good.

> *And we know that all things work together for good to them that love God, to them who are called according to his purpose.* **Romans 8:28**

I know there are times in our lives when God allows a trial to come our way, even when life seems to be in total concert with God's will for us. A trial can come during a time when we feel we have surrendered all to Him, a time when we feel we are being led by the Spirit of the Lord rather than relying on our own understanding. It can be difficult for us to rationalize why God would allow something bad to happen to us at a time of our greatest intimacy with Him.

What we fail to understand is that it is during these times of closeness with the Lord that we become vessels He can use to give glory to His Holy name. This glory comes by showing other believers and the world that the God we serve is a God of all seasons, during the good times and during the bad times. He is a God during the times when we feel like we are on top of the mountain and when we feel we are in the depths of our valley. No matter where we are, He is still God!

> *Whither shall I go from thy spirit? Or whither shall I flee from thy presence? If I ascend up into heaven thou art there: if I make my bed in hell, behold thou art there. If I take the wings of the morning, and dwell in the uttermost parts of the sea; Even there shall thy hand lead me, and thy right hand shall hold me. If I say, Surely the darkness*

*shall cover me; even the night shall be
light about me.* **Psalms 139:7-11**

This season of uncertainties has afforded me the opportunity to face faith head-on and unfiltered—there is no one in the ring but faith and me. I have looked faith straight in the eye; I have stood firm in my belief in God's Word and have continued to live my life based on God's unseen promises. Faith has challenged my resolve and my ability to continue to be steadfast and immovable in the faith of Jesus Christ. I have not turned my back on God, nor have I sought consolation from the world. I have not blamed anyone for my situation, even though there have been opportunities to blame others. I have remained upbeat and positive, continuing to view my situation based on what it will become as opposed to what it is today. Standing in the ring alone with faith, I have been hit with some heavy blows, but I have not gone down; each blow has made me even stronger and more resolute in my relationship with and belief in Jesus Christ. I have continued to look to the Lord for direction, as He is the author and finisher of my faith.

Casting all your care upon him; for he careth for you. *1 Peter 5:7*

Trust in the Lord with all thine heart; and lean not unto thine own understanding.

> In all thy ways acknowledge him, and
> he shall direct thy paths. ***Proverbs 3:5-6***

I have been in the ring with faith for about fifteen months now, and God has rendered a unanimous decision: I have been declared to have "real faith"! To God be the glory! I am committed, I will not quit, I will not throw in the towel, I will not give up, I will not lie down, I will not surrender to the world, and I will not stop serving the Lord in spirit and in truth.

> For I am persuaded; that neither death, nor life, nor angels, nor principalities, nor powers, nor things present, nor things to come, Nor height, nor depth, nor any other creature, shall be able to separate us from the love of God, which is in Christ Jesus our Lord. ***Romans 8:38-39***

All Things Working
For My Good

As a believer, I have come to accept the promises of God as absolute truth. As a child of God, born again by His Spirit, I enjoy a relationship with Christ as His child rather than just as His creation. Being born of His Spirit means I have heard the true gospel of Jesus Christ and believe in my heart and have reconciled in my mind that Jesus Christ is the Son of God. Jesus was manifested as a human and gave up His life on the cross for my sins; He defeated death and rose again to reign in heaven with God the Father. My relationship with Christ allows me to love God in a way that defies human logic and understanding. The Spirit of God gives me, as a true believer, faith beyond human reasoning, thus allowing me to see things through spiritual eyes rather than fleshly eyes. As a true believer, I can see things as they will be based on the promises of God rather than how they currently appear.

My relationship with Christ gives me the confidence to live my life based on God's promises rather than by my current circumstances. As a true believer, I know that life's situations do not define my relationship with Christ, but rather my relationship with Christ gives greater meaning to my life. As a true believer, I can rise above my trials and challenges to see what is possible beyond my current season of uncertainties.

> *And hath raised us up together, and made us sit together in heavenly places in Christ Jesus: (7) That in the ages to come he might show the exceeding riches of his grace in his kindness toward us through Christ Jesus.* **Ephesians 2:6-7**

> *For we walk by faith, not by sight*: **2 Corinthians 5:7**

I know there are times in life's journey when we just don't understand why we must endure such hardships, trials, and disappointments. During these difficult times, we must come to a place in our relationship with Christ where we accept by faith that everything will work out for our good if we just keep our life aligned with God and stay connected to Him. God created us in His image for worship and to give His holy name all glory and honor. Sometimes God uses hardships in our lives for His purpose and to ultimately give His holy name glory and honor.

Draw nigh to God, and he will draw nigh to you. Cleanse your hands, ye sinners; and purify your hearts, ye double-minded. **James 4:8**

Abide in me, and I in you, As the branch cannot bear fruit of itself, except it abide in the vine; no more can ye, except ye abide in me. (5) I am the vine, ye are the branches: He that abideth in me and I in him, the same bringeth forth much fruit: for without me ye can do nothing. **John 15:4-5**

Behold, I have refined thee, but not with silver; I have chosen thee in the furnace of affliction. (11) For mine own sake, even for mine own sake, will I do it: for how should my name be polluted? And I will not give my glory unto another. **Isaiah 48:10-11**

What Is This Good That God Is Doing On My Behalf?

When we are facing a difficult challenge, people who are not experiencing current crises in their lives often tell us that we should hold on and stay positive. They say that as believers, we should know and accept that God works all things for our good. All of this sounds good; however, it takes more than just words to be able to stand firm when something has just turned your life seemingly upside down. Words alone are not enough; we must be at a place in our lives and relationships with our Savior where we know without doubt or wavering that God has our best interest at heart. In other words, we must feel the assurances from God that in time, He will work out to our benefit whatever this thing is that is causing us concern as we continue to journey through our earthly lives.

What is this good that God promises me? In order to accept and believe God's promises, I must first gain a proper understating of them. When God tells

His children living within His will that He will work whatever we are going through for our good, it does not mean He will grant us everything we want and at the time we want it. In some health crises, it may not be God's will to heal our earthly body, or in other cases, it may not be His will to bail us out of a difficult situation. What He has promised is that He will use whatever we are going through to make us more acceptable to Him and that the results will give His Holy name glory.

> And we know that all things work together for good to them that love God, to them who are called according to *his* purpose. **Romans 8:28**

This good that God promises me is that He will be with me every step of the way, that whatever comes my way will not jeopardize His promise of eternal life, to be with Him in Heaven forever. Sometimes God heals us of cancer or other illnesses to show the world who He is, to encourage His children to stay the course and remain steadfast. Other times God gives us the strength and endurance to continue to worship and serve Him regardless of our individual challenges or circumstances. It is during these times that the Name of Jesus is lifted up and glorified on earth.

But what is "good"? We can look at good from three perspectives. The first type of good is worldly good, which is nothing more than things that are temporal and have no lasting or permanent value. The second is spiritual good, which includes things that add real spiritual value to our earthly lives and prepare us for eternal life, making us more acceptable to God. The third good is eternal good, which are things that are everlasting and offer abiding fellowship with God forever.

I know with certainty that in the end, God will work out whatever I am going through for my good; it may not be what I have requested or expected, but it will be for my good. Those who do not have a personal relationship with God cannot understand or comprehend how a loving God can work things out in our lives for our good without physically healing us or granting us the desires of our heart. However, I know that sometimes my wishes and my desires simply don't line up with God's will for my life. I also know that God's will for my life is far better than my desires, because the manifestation of His will in my life makes me more acceptable to Him.

It is impossible to understand how God is working on my behalf or for my good when there is no earthly manifestation of any visible results of this good. God certainly can, and may, manifest physical healing and transformation of my physical body. However, the primary transformation that is taking place within me during this crisis is not physical but spiritual. I feel a deeper sense of the presence of God, allowing me a clearer perspective of who God is, which has increased my faith in God and His promises. I am now able to surrender all my concerns and problems to the Lord, who cares for me.

Getting To Know God Up Close And Personal

During this season of my life, I have been placed in a position where I had to decide whether to trust God or just give up. I chose to fully trust Him, believing He will deliver on everything He has promised. The statistics and data related to my health condition do not align themselves with the promises God has made to me. Fortunately, I have come to believe God is more powerful than any statistic or data, and I know He specializes in accomplishing what is impossible to man. There is still a lot of growth that needs to take place in me; my desire is to get to a place where I trust God completely, without any doubt, wavering, or hesitation.

> *Now faith is the substance of things hoped for, the evidence of things not seen.* **Hebrews 11:1**

I know this sounds very strange; however, I feel as if God has given me a gift—an opportunity to connect with Him at a level of intimacy I never could have imagined prior to this personal crisis. I call this space where I am now ***getting to know God up close and personal***. When I now communicate with God in prayer, I feel as if I am giving Him all of me; I have no desire to hold back anything from Him. I know God already knows everything about me, but sometimes, as human creatures, we are reluctant to share the deep, intimate part of who we are—the innermost part of who we *really* are, not just who we say we are. We are motivated to look at ourselves in a mirror with spiritual eyes rather than fleshly eyes—seeing ourselves the way God sees us, with no need to pretend we are anything other than who we are. If there is one person to whom we should be willing to reveal ourselves, it should be God! God wants to help us, to heal our deep, hidden wounds that have been untreated for years and are negatively affecting our spiritual well-being.

> *But we all, with open face beholding*
> *as in a glass the glory of the Lord, are*
> *changed into the same image from glory*
> *to glory, even as by the Spirit of the Lord.*
> ***2 Corinthians 3:18***

When I revealed to God the innermost intimacy of my spiritual condition, this openness with Him allowed me to experience a greater evolution of surrendering myself to the will of God and accepting His will for my life. Since I was revealing all to God, I had less desire to hold on to things I should have already given to Him a long time ago. I felt lighter than I had ever felt; no part of my life was holding me back from accomplishing all that God has assigned me to do. It's like living out the Word of God, "If any man be in Christ, he is a new creature."

> *Therefore if any man be in Christ, he is a new creature: old things are passed away; behold, all things are become new.* ***2 Corinthians 5:17***
>
> *But Jesus beheld them, and said unto them, with men this is impossible; but with God all things are possible.* ***Matthew 19:26***

Over the past ten to fifteen years, I have considered myself to be a person who surrendered most, if not all, to God. Well, during this season, I have realized that I was still holding on to areas in my life that I thought I had released to God. Gaining greater and deeper intimacy with God has allowed me to see what I could not see prior to this season. I have come to a place of acceptance in my life; I now know that whatever happens to me is totally dependent on the grace, mercy, favor, and compassion of a loving God. So there is no logical reason to hold anything back from Him.

> *I thou prepare thine heart, and stretch out thine hands toward him; If iniquity be in thine hand, put it far away, and let not wickedness dwell in thy tabernacles. For then shalt thou lift up thy face without spot; yea, thou shalt be steadfast, and shalt not fear:* **Job 11:13-15**

My desire is to be more like Jesus every day. I know I will never be a perfect individual, because there is only one who is perfect, and that is the Son of God, Jesus Christ. However, I will continue to strive to be more Christlike as I journey here on earth.

> *And be not conformed to this world: but be ye transformed by the renewing of your mind, that ye may prove what is that good, and acceptable, and perfect, will of God.* **Romans 12:2**

Receiving What God
Has For Me

I have come to accept and embrace that God has something He desires me to receive that I can only get by traveling down this new path on which He has placed me. I believe this season of earthly uncertainties will serve to further define or enhance my ministry and add deeper clarity to God's call on my life. I believe that what I am lacking in my ministry today can only come through trusting God during this difficult and uncertain period. I believe God will use these current challenges and trials to pull me even closer to Him. As I get closer to God and gain greater intimacy with Him, then I will be able to hear His voice in a way I have never heard Him before. I believe the clarity of His voice will give me a deeper understanding of *His* call for my life and ministry. I further believe that this period of greater intimacy will foster greater illumination of God's Word and truths, which I so deeply desire.

I now have a much more comprehensive appreciation of what the apostle Paul was referring to when he spoke about his thorn in the flesh and why God would not remove it from him, even though he had made a petition to God on several occasions to remove it. The Bible does not tell us exactly what Paul's thorn in the flesh was; however, we do know it kept Paul well grounded and did not allow him to get puffed up with pride. This thorn, or physical challenge, in Paul's life kept him humble and full of humility. Paul's physical challenges served to remind him that his ministry and accomplishments were all about God and never about him. Paul states that if it were not for this thorn in his flesh, he might have started to believe it was about him, and if that were to happen, he would no longer have been an effective minister of the gospel of Jesus Christ. Paul realized God did not need his physicality but rather his spirituality; in other words, when Paul was physically weak, the Spirit of God made him strong.

> *And lest I should be exalted above measure through the abundance of the revelations, there was given to me a thorn in the flesh, the messenger of Satan to buffet me, lest I should be exalted above measure. For this thing I besought the Lord thrice, that it might depart from me. And he said unto me, My grace is sufficient for thee: for my strength is made*

*perfect in weakness. Most gladly there-
fore will I rather glory in my infirmities,
that the power of Christ may rest upon
me. Therefore I take pleasure in infirmities, in reproaches, in necessities, in
persecutions, in distresses for Christ's
sake: for when I am weak, then am I
strong.* **2 Corinthians 12:7-10**

As difficult as it may sometimes seem, our suffering,
trials, and tribulations are nothing more than tools for
the enhancement of our ministry. Thorns in the flesh—
whether physical or mental—are brought on God's mes-
sengers by the powers of Satan, but God allows them
for our good. When we can continue to remain steadfast
and immovable in the mist of our suffering, God gets
His glory from our ministry.

*Therefore, my beloved brethren, be ye
steadfast, unmovable, always abounding
in the work of the Lord, forasmuch as ye
know that your labor is not in vain in the
Lord.* **1 Corinthians 15:58**

When a believer of Jesus Christ can rise above personal challenges and continue to be steadfast in his or
her praise and worship to the one true God, this gives
honor and reverence to His name. God is not only
pleased, but His holy name is lifted for all to see, and

thus God gets His glory through our resolve. We can show the world that we are still standing, not by our own might but by the power of God that is in us.

> *Ye are of God, little children, and have overcome them: because greater is he that is in you, than he that is in the world.* **1 John 4:4**

When Life Hits You With An Unexpected Turn

Wow, cancer has entered my life.

Over my life's journey, I have had minor health challenges before but never one that was considered life-threatening. Most only required a brief period of rehabilitation or healing. However, my current situation threatens my earthly existence, so God, I am trusting and leaning on You. I understand the physical seriousness of my illness, but I also know the awesomeness of Your power. I have seen Your handiwork, and I am convinced beyond any doubt that there is nothing You cannot do if it is Your will. So, my faith has grown even stronger since this season of cancer began almost a year ago. When this journey started, You promised me that if I would place all my trust in You and lean not on my own understanding, this season would not limit my ability to take on and complete every task You would assign me to do. I have not only been able to honor my call as a pastor, a preacher, and a teacher of the gospel, but by Your grace, I have also been able to accept more outside preaching engagements during this season than I have in prior years. ***You are truly a mighty God!***

> *And he said unto me, My grace is suffi-*
> *cient for thee: for my strength is made*
> *perfect in weakness. Most gladly there-*
> *fore will I rather glory in my infirmities,*
> *that the power of Christ may rest upon*
> *me.* ***2 Corinthians 12:9***

The side effects of my illness that the doctors warned me about have not manifested themselves beyond the regular occurrence of severe hot flashes. However, since I am a person who does not normally perspire much, most people beyond my immediate family have not recognized any physical change in my health. Thank God!

In late October 2018, while preparing for my annual travels to St. Lucia, West Indies, to attend a local pastors' conference, I went through my normal yearly physical examination in preparation for the trip. When my blood-work came back, the results showed I could potentially have cancer. The results were so high that the doctor felt the reading may in fact have been a system error. As a result, he ordered more conclusive tests, including a biopsy, to determine what was really happening. In late January 2019, all the tests were completed, and the results were documented. At this time, I was informed that I had cancer. After several more visits to the doctor, it was determined that my cancer was very severe and considered to be stage 4. At this point, I was told that the only feasible medical option for me was radiation, since the doctors did not believe surgery was viable for me due to the extent of the cancer in the affected area of my body. However, I knew with absolute certainty that my best option was to trust in the power of a loving and merciful God, Jesus Christ.

I really did not want to have surgery; I simply did not want them cutting into the cancer. After learning the news, I immediately started doing my own personal research on stage 4 cancer; I read everything I could fine on the Internet. I also contacted the Med Star Cancer Center of Philadelphia to seek a third opinion, since Kaiser and Virginia Medical Center had already rendered their conclusions. After providing them with the results of my prior tests and after several conference calls, they agreed with the findings and the recommendation from Kaiser and Virginia Medical Center in Arlington, Virginia.

By the grace of God, I met with a cancer specialist with the Virginia Medical Center, and we created a radiation plan just for me. It consisted of about four months of intense, focused radiation and a few weeks of very intensive radiation called Cyber Knife Radiation, a stereotactic body radiation therapy device that delivers radiation using advanced imaging technology. I was very blessed that I did not experience any real side effects from the radiation. In fact, during the period I received radiation—which took place at 10:00 a.m. every morning Monday through Friday—my treatment never hindered my pastoral duties and obligations. It was truly amazing to experience in real time the goodness and mercy of a loving God.

When I learned for sure that I did indeed have cancer, I made up in my mind that I would not tell anyone except my wife. I remember how difficult it was to tell my wife of almost fifty years, because I had never envisioned cancer being part of our journey together. I was concerned about how this news might affect my wife's health; I did not want her to suffer physically or mentally because of my own health challenges. However, I soon recalled what I have often preached: sometimes bad things happen to us during our journey in life that are totally beyond our control. My first reaction was to take inventory of my life and my walk with the Lord to make sure this cancer was not the result of sin or disobedience. I am a preacher of the gospel, but I am not a perfect man; nor am I without sin. However, I knew of no sin or act of rebellion or disobedience that was part of my walk with Christ. Over the past thirty years or so, my journey has been one of steadfast faith and increasing surrender to God's will for my life. In fact, I believe that my spirituality and obedience to God's will are at their highest point of my earthly existence, yet I am far from perfect!

So why had cancer entered my life at this season and with such ferocity? As I went to the Word of God to gain a biblical perspective of what was happening, I quickly realized I was going through a season of faith testing, commitment, endurance, and steadfastness.

> *Being confident of this very thing, that he which hath begun a good work in you will perform it until the day of Jesus Christ.* ***Philippians 1:6***

Over the past few years, I have come to believe and accept that God has called me to boldly preach the true gospel in a time when so many preachers are watering down the true Word of God to make it more acceptable to the world. I have been called to preach the full council of God's Word—both the blessings and the curses—without adding or subtracting from God's inspired Word.

> *Preach the word; be instant in season, out of season; reprove, rebuke, exhort with all longsuffering and doctrine.* ***2 Timothy 4:2***

> *For I have not shunned to declare unto you all the counsel of God. (28) Take heed therefore unto yourselves, and to all the flock, over the which the Holy Ghost hath made you overseers, to feed the church of God, which he hath purchased with his own blood.* ***Acts 20:27-28***

The true Word of God is not very popular today, for it goes against our worldly lifestyle. Our worldly desires have caused this generation to serve the creature more than the Creator. From the Word of God, we know that the devil—yes, old Satan himself—is the god of this world for a season. We also know he has blinded the minds of those who are lost and who have not accepted the free gift of eternal life by acknowledging, believing in, and receiving by faith the redeeming power of Jesus Christ.

> *In whom the god of this world hath blinded the minds of them which believe not, lest the light of the glorious gospel of Christ, who is the image of God, should shine unto them.* **2 Corinthians 4:4**

I am fully aware that the false god of this world, Satan, seeks to stop me from preaching the inspired Word of God. However, I know that He who is in me is greater than he who is in the world, so I realize that whatever God has allowed me to start, He will enable me to complete it through His might and power. Most importantly, Satan cannot harm me unless God allows him to do so, and if God allows this, then it will be for my good and the name of our Lord will be lifted up and glorified for all to see.

A Season Of Introspection

Some might wonder why I chose not to share my illness with my church family. I did consider sharing my condition with them; however, I did not want to take the risk of slowing down or stopping the spiritual momentum that our church was (and still is!) experiencing here at St. John through a move of the Holy Spirit. God is doing some amazing things in the lives of our members: individual lives are being transformed, relationships are being mended, old wounds are being healed, failed health is being restored, and most of all, each week, people are growing closer to the Lord.

Some might consider my excuse somewhat selfish, but I simply did not want my members, who had always shown me and my family tremendous love, to take their eyes off the target and start worrying about their pastor. They were already covering me with their love and prayers. More than a year ago, God called the church to set up groups of prayer warriors to pray for potential vulnerable areas or work within the church. By a move of the Holy Spirit, we were led to create eighteen prayer groups known as Prayer Platoons. Each day, these Prayer Platoons pray for a specific area or work in the church, and once a week, they come together as a unit for corporate prayer. There is no doubt in my mind that the favor and success that the Lord has bestowed upon me, my family, and our church are direct results of the consistent and fervent prayers of our dedicated members.

In fact, we have a Prayer Platoon known as the Shepherd Prayer Platoon that prays for me, my health, my family, and my ministry every day. They are already doing what God called them to do for their pastor. I have also gone before the throne of God on my own behalf, and I believe without any reservation or doubt that God has heard my petition. My faith and resolve have allowed me to continue to carry out my day-to-day responsibilities and activities as if I have already been completely healed. Through prayer and fasting, I have complete and unwavering faith in the promises of God. I believe He will allow me to complete every task He has assigned me to do. In short, my health situation will not interfere with my spiritual assignments. I am of the mindset that my current health challenges have invigorated—and will continue to invigorate—my ministry, and they have certainly given me a sense of urgency.

Now faith is the substance of things hoped for, the evidence of things not seen. *Hebrews 11:1*

But without faith it is impossible to please him: for he that cometh to God must believe that he is, and that he is a rewarder of them that diligently seek him. *Hebrews 11:6*

If my people, which are called by my name, shall humble themselves, and pray, and seek my face, and turn from their wicked ways; then will I hear from heaven, and will forgive their sin, and will heal their land. *2 Chronicles 7:14*

Confess your faults one to another, and pray one for another, that ye may be healed. The effectual fervent prayer of the righteous man availeth much. *James 5:16*

And he spoke a parable unto them to this end, that men ought always to pray, and not to faint. *Luke 18:1*

Through prayer, I have witnessed some miraculous transformations of people and circumstances. I have witnessed family members and friends coming out of the world of darkness and experiencing the marvelous light of salvation through a new walk with Jesus Christ. I have also witnessed brothers and sisters stand and take accountability for their lives and their relationships with Christ, and stop blaming the world and everybody else for their failures and their disappointments. But most of all, I have seen the power of God move upon the lives of believers, and as a result, God has transported them from a place of no hope to a place of true faith in Him and His ability to fulfill all the promises He has made to them. The growth of our faithful members over that past year or so has been nothing short of breathtaking.

The Grace Of God

At this time in my life, I believe I have become more deeply involved in my ministry from a spiritual standpoint. I have always considered myself to be a compassionate and committed preacher, teacher, and pastor. However, in this current season, I feel an even greater passion and commitment to my spiritual calling. It is as if God has granted me an extra measure of grace for such a time as this. I am not the only one affected by this extra grace; I have witnessed the spiritual growth of my members here at St. John as well. Their commitment and dedication to their assigned ministries has been astonishing. I have also seen real change in the lives of my members. Through the power of God, I have witnessed marriages being reconciled and strengthened, deep-rooted spiritual strongholds being broken down, and members' lives being set free from sin that had hindered their spiritual growth and maturity.

Time and time again, I have also witnessed our members surrendering more of their will to God and then experiencing greater victory in their lives. The dedication, commitment, and personal sacrifices to the work of God from individual members within the body of St. John have reached consistently high levels. This is not because of me but because of the power and presence of the Holy Spirit in their lives. It is as if somebody turned on a spiritual switch. I can feel in my spirit that this growth is not superficial; it will sustain itself over time. This type of growth has fostered a stronger spiritual foundation for the church, as well as for individual members and families.

> But unto every one of us is given grace according to the measure of the gift of Christ. *Ephesians 4:7*

I know in my heart that all of this is the result of an extra measure of grace from a loving God; without His grace, none of this would have manifested. I also know God expects more from me and St. John during this season of abundant grace. God did not give us this extra grace so we could just sit back and rest on our past efforts; He has given us this grace to help us go out and reach the lost and lead them to salvation through the furtherance of the gospel. Although we are a small church, through the grace of God, our size has not hindered our ability to share the gospel in several countries outside the borders of the United States. God's grace allows us to support missionary work in Haiti; St. Lucia, West Indies; St. Vincent, West Indies; Dominica, West Indies; Granada, West Indies; and other Caribbean Islands.

For the perfecting of the saints for the work of the ministry for the edifying of the body of Christ: Till we all come in the unity of the faith, and of the knowledge of the Son of God, unto a perfect man, unto the measure of the stature of the fullness of Christ: *Ephesians 4:12-13*

Now God is calling St. John and me to greater outreach—not only outside our country's borders but within its walls as well. As a small church, we have limited resources; however, God has given the church and me an extra measure of grace for such a time as this. We know and believe that we serve an arisen God who can do anything except fall. We have faith that if we stay connected to God, He will provide for all our needs. During this season, it is our objective to ensure that each of our members shares the gospel with each of his or her immediate family members. We are seeking God's grace and mercy with spiritual boldness and asking Him to save all our church members' immediate family. We realize this is an extremely bold request, but we also know that we serve a mighty God who firmly stated in His Word that nothing is impossible for Him if we just believe and have faith. We have made a commitment to trust God completely and to be steadfast and immovable in our service to the Lord.

> Therefore, my beloved brethren, be ye steadfast, unmovable, always abounding in the work of the Lord, forasmuch as ye know that your labor is not in vain in the Lord. *1 Corinthians 15:58*

Getting Back Up And Staying On Course

When God allowed this unexpected detour in my life's journey, it never crossed my mind to stop following Him, nor did I stop seeking His divine guidance for my life. I quickly came to the realization that everything was going to be all right and I would be OK if I just embraced this season in faith and trust, with great anticipation of what God was going to do in my life and in my ministry. Embracing this current season meant I had to come to a place of accepting that my situation was nothing more than a season that would soon pass by.

However, embracing this season has had its challenges. There are times when Satan tries to deceive me by whispering lies in my ear, telling me that God does not really love or care for me the way I think He does. Satan whispers words such as, "Charles, you have devoted your life to Christ and the spreading of the gospel, and look at what it's gotten you. Cancer!"

During this same period, however, the Holy Spirit has reminded me that I am more than a conqueror through Jesus Christ and that everything will work out in the end for my good. I am able to boldly proclaim that neither death nor life shall separate me from the Love of God. I thank God that I am able to discern His voice from the voice of a liar and a deceiver who wants to steal, kill, and destroy my soul. Satan tried this same tactic on Jesus when He was in the wilderness. That tactic did not work then, and it will not work now, for I am a child of the living God. When Satan tries these deceptive tactics, I tell him to get thee behind me, that I worship and serve the Lord only. During this season, I remain faithful and steadfast in my relationship with the Lord. I pledge as much as is within me to never doubt that God is working on my behalf to turn my current season into something that will be for my good and will give His holy Name glory.

> For I am persuaded, that neither death, nor life, nor angels, nor principalities, nor powers, nor things present, nor things to come, Nor height, nor depth, nor any other creature, shall be able to separate us from the love of God, which is in Christ Jesus our Lord.
> ***Romans 8:38-39***

> And Jesus answered and said unto him,
> Get thee behind me, Satan: for it is
> written, THOU SHALT WORSHIP THE
> LORD THY GOD, AND HIM ONLY
> SHALT THOU SERVE. *Luke 4:8*

I love my wife and my family very much; they are very important to me. However, my commitment and dedication to the call of God takes priority over everything else in my life!

I know this sounds strange considering my current situation, but I am excited and humbled for the Lord to use me as His vessel at such a time as this. It is my prayer that God might give me just a little of the spiritual fortitude He gave Jeremiah and many great men of the Bible. I am by no means attempting to put myself in the same category as Jeremiah or any other great man of Scripture; I am just an old preacher trying to do the best I can considering my limited biblical knowledge.

God has used the following examples to remind me that He sometimes allows suffering, trials, and trying situations in the lives of His servants to do His will and work as well as to give glory to His Name. He called Jeremiah, who wrote the Book of Jeremiah, to prophesy during the reign of Judah's last king, King Zedekiah, during the final decade of the Southern Kingdom. Jeremiah was deeply spiritual and totally committed to God; despite his personal struggles, his love for God and God's people never ceased. The remorse Jeremiah felt delivering a message of condemnation against Judah caused him to have doubt about his ability to honor God's call. As a result, Jeremiah struggled in his ministry with feelings of rejection, loneliness and isolation because of the harshness of the message. Jeremiah was a prophet whose heart was filled with pain. Jeremiah's struggles were both personal and spiritual yet through it all he remained faithful to God's call. Jeremiah's life and ministry remind us that those who are called may struggle in their assignment, but the power of God will sustain them, if they stay focused and connected to God.

Jeremiah's love for God encouraged him to be courageous in the face of severe opposition and tragic circumstances. Although Jeremiah was severely persecuted by his own people, he knew that God Almighty was in total control and that God had a plan.

> For I know the thoughts that I think toward you, saith the Lord, thoughts of peace, and not of evil, to give you an expected end. **Jeremiah 29:11**

In the Bible, there are many other examples of men who did not allow their situations or circumstances to hinder the call God placed on their lives or their love for God's people. The apostle Paul wrote many of the New Testament epistles while locked in a Roman jail cell. However, he never allowed his circumstances to hinder what God had called him to do. The apostle Paul was willing to suffer persecution for the furtherance of the gospel. Paul's desire to see people saved and come to the full knowledge of Jesus Christ and His redeeming power was a greater priority than his earthly circumstances.

As I look at the lives of these great men of faith, they encourage me to believe that in some small way, I too might have the opportunity to be used by God for the furtherance of the gospel during my minor health challenge.

Undeserved Mercy

The joy that I feel just being allowed to see another day is truly magnificent!

My current season has taught me to embrace the moment more and to enjoy what God is doing for me right now. I have always been a person who truly enjoys life and living; I have never spent much time complaining about anything. At a very young age, I learned from my father and mother to be thankful of what I have rather than complaining about what I don't have. My father and mother were strong, God-fearing people who would often tell my siblings and me that we should count our blessings and thank God for what He had given us.

As a result, I grew up being appreciative of what we had in the home. As a young boy and as an adult, I would never compare what I had or did not have to anyone else. My parents taught my siblings and me not to be envious of anyone or anything. If I wanted something, I knew I had to work hard and be willing to make personal sacrifices to get what I wanted. I believed that if I was honest and worked hard, there were no limits to what I could achieve. I never considered myself to be overly gifted, but I was extremely motivated.

My current season has given me a renewed appreciation for embracing the moment. I know that each day is a gift from God; however, prior to this season, I lived my life as if tomorrow and the next day would come. Well, now I do not assume anything; I embrace each day as a gift all by itself. I try not to make it contingent upon the next day. I just try to enjoy the blessings and beauty of this day. This mindset has allowed me to get the maximum enjoyment out of every aspect of my life each day. When I wake in the morning, the first thing I do is thank God for the gift of this day. I understand how precious this day is, and I am thankful to have received this gift. I have learned to embrace the elements of each gifted day, both the good and the not-so-good.

> It is of the Lord's mercies that we are not consumed, because his compassions fail not. They are new every morning: great is the faithfulness. *Lamentations 3:22-23*

When I wake up and see my wife's face, I get very emotional inside because I realize God has given me the gift of being with her for one more day. When I see my daughter, my heart jumps because God has given me the gift of seeing and loving her for one more day. Almost every day, I usually communicate with my three sons in some form or another, and when I connect with them, even if by text, there is such a rush that goes through me that gives me joy. I feel the same when one of my grandchildren calls or stops by; what a gift! When I speak with other members of my family, what a gift from God that is. When I see or speak with one of my church members, what a gift from God that is as well.

When I preach or share the gospel with someone, I realize this opportunity is a gift from God, so I try to make the most out of the moment. In other words, I try to give it all I have. I have come to realize and accept that each day is a personal gift from God—one we did not desire but was given by a loving and merciful God. No one but God knows when this gift of life will stop, so I have decided to embrace fully and without reservation every moment of every day with a heart of thanksgiving!

> God is our refuge and strength, a very present help in trouble. *Psalms 46:1*

> The name of the Lord is a strong tower: the righteous runneth into it, and is safe. *Proverbs 18:10*

A Joy And Peace Beyond Human Understanding

This season of unexpected challenges and uncertainties has fostered inner peace and joy in my life that far exceeds human reasoning. For most people, it may be difficult to understand and accept the peace and joy I am experiencing, for this is a peace and joy that defy human logic. It's a divine peace and joy that can only come from a loving God.

> Come unto me all ye that labor and are heavy laden, and I will give you rest. Take my yoke upon you, and learn of me; for I am meek and lowly in heart: and ye shall find rest unto your souls. For my yoke is easy, and my burden is light. *Matthew 11:28-30*

My heightened sense of the presence of God in my life has allowed me to cast all my cares, concerns, uncertainties, and burdens on the Lord, for I know He cares for me. In prior years, this type of challenge might have added additional worry to my life, but now that my worries have been placed in the hands of a loving God, I am at total peace. I am free to enjoy my life without worrying about my situation. My only requirement is to be obedient to God and to live according to His commandments to the best of my spiritual ability.

> Be careful for nothing; but in every thing by prayer and supplication with thanksgiving let your requests be known unto God. And the peace of God, which passeth all understanding, shall keep your hearts and minds through Christ Jesus. *Philippians 4:6-7*

> Let this mind be in you, which was also in Christ Jesus. *Philippians 2:5*

I know from the Word of God that God has a plan for my life of good and not evil. If I live my life in accordance with the precepts of God, I believe God's plan will be manifested. I have undeniable faith that God will grant me enough time to complete every task He has assigned me to do. I believe that the only way any assigned task will not be completed is through disobedience. For this reason, I pray daily that the Lord will give me a greater capacity to surrender my will and desires and to embrace His will for my life.

> For I know the thoughts that I think
> toward you, saith the Lord, thoughts of
> peace, and not of evil, to give you an
> expected end. Then shall ye call upon
> me, and ye shall go and pray unto me,
> and I will hearken unto you. And ye
> shall seek me, and find me, when ye
> shall search for me with all your heart.
> *Jeremiah 29:11-13*

I have spent considerable time alone trying to assess my current mindset with my mindset from earlier years in my life. In the past, I could not have imagined the positions or mindset that I now wholeheartedly embrace. This mindset that now guides my thinking and beliefs can only be embraced from a spiritual perspective rather than a human or fleshly perspective. My current mindset is the result of feeding my spirit the Word of God rather than feeding my flesh the spirit of darkness and deception. Currently, in my life, I know without a doubt that greater is He that is in me than he that is in the world.

> I am crucified with Christ: nevertheless
> I live; yet not I, but Christ liveth in me:
> and the life which I now live in the flesh

I live by the faith of the Son of God,
who loved me, and gave himself for me.
Galatians 2:20

Therefore if any man be in Christ, he
is a new creature: old things are passed
away; behold, all things are become
new. *2 Corinthians 5:17*

Looking Forward

While I continue in my present season of challenges and earthly uncertainties, I am looking beyond this season and focusing more on the next. Although my next season has not yet been identified, I know in my heart that it very much exists and that it will be manifested at the appropriate time. God's plan for my life and ministry is still unfolding; there are still many mountains to climb, seas to cross, and valleys to overcome.

Even though God has not yet revealed my next season, I remain excited about the possibility of continuing the work that He has assigned me to do here at the St. John Baptist Church. My eyes and my heart are focused on things that are in front of me rather than things that are behind me. I consider this present season to be behind me; even though it has not been medically concluded, it is resolved!

> I press toward the mark for the prize of
> the high calling of God in Christ Jesus.
> *Philippians 3:14*

My eagerness to continue to serve God in whatever capacity He desires remains my highest priority. Today, I feel better prepared for future assignments from God than I had felt prior to my season of health challenges. I have now come to believe that my season of challenges and uncertainties was in actuality a period of preparation for future ministry growth and assignments.

> Being confident of this very thing, that
> he which hath begun a good work in
> your will perform it until the day of
> Jesus Christ: *Philippians 1:6*

Although I am very much prepared to answer the call of the Lord whenever He calls me home, I continue to believe there remains much work and living to be done here on earth. I believe the Lord has promised me many more days and years of loving companionship with my wife of more than fifty years, Ruby. I cherish each day the Lord allows me to wake up, look into her eyes, and reflect on all the love and joy He has bestowed on our life together. Truly, we have benefitted from an extra measure of grace from a loving God.

> But unto every one of us is given grace
> according to the measure of the gift of
> Christ. *Ephesians 4:7*

I look forward to witnessing the continued maturation of my sons into the men God has called them to be. I am very proud of the men they have become however, I know the best is yet to come. My life has been enriched by God's gift of grandchildren, especially as I have witnessed their growth in their early years as well as from adolescence to adulthood.

I believe God has promised me the pleasure and joy of being able not only to walk my only daughter down the aisle of her marriage but to perform the ceremony as well. I have been extremely blessed to perform the marriage ceremonies for two of our sons, but to walk my only daughter down the aisle will be special. What a day that will be!

> For all the promises of God in him are
> yea, and in him Amen, unto the glory of
> God by us. *2 Corinthians 1:20*

There are still lots of family gatherings and reunions that will take place here on earth before our family reunion in heaven. I look forward to the fellowship, love, and fun that will be shared in the coming weeks, months, and years.

And we know that all things work together for good to them that love God, to them who are the called according to his purpose. *Romans 8:28*

Somebody say . . . "Jesus"!!

Thank God I Have
Been Healed

It has been about fifteen months since my first cancer diagnosis, and I have completed most of my health treatment plan. At this time, I am boldly declaring that I am healed by the power of God. I believe by faith that my body is completely cancer-free. I have not yet heard this from my doctors, but I have heard it in my spirit. I live by the Spirit of God, not by flesh. I don't know when the full manifestation of my healing will take place; it really does not matter, because I am healed. I have made a conscious decision to live my life based on the promise of God—that He will never leave or forsake me.

I thank God for giving ear to my petition and for granting me grace and mercy in the midst of my cry.

> A merry heart doeth good like medicine: but a broken spirit drieth the bones.
> *Proverbs 17:22*

About the Author

Charles A. Hall

Charles A. Hall, a servant of Jesus Christ, has been in the ministry for more than twenty years. He is currently the pastor of St. John Baptist Church of Alexandria, Virginia, where he has served for the past eight years.

Pastor Hall resides with his helpmate and wife, Ruby, with whom he has enjoyed more than fifty years of marriage. Together, the couple has raised and educated four children and is blessed with four grandchildren.

Pastor Hall's parents, Charles and Luella Hall, were a major influence on his relationship with the Lord; they introduced him to the Lord at a very early age. While his journey in life led him in many different directions, he never lost his connection to the Lord. Pastor Hall is a committed family man and is passionate about sharing the gospel to all who will hear.

CPSIA information can be obtained
at www.ICGtesting.com
Printed in the USA
FSHW011948060820
72740FS